ACROSS THE DARK

poems by
Pam Bernard

Main Street Rag Publishing Co.
Charlotte, NC

Please direct all inquiries to:

Main Street Rag Publishing Company
PO BOX 691621
Charlotte, NC 28227-7028
w w w . M a i n S t r e e t R a g . c o m

Library of Congress
Catalog Card Number: 2002112734
ISBN.1-930907-0851400
Cover painting by Pam Bernard
Cover design by Pam & Harry Bernard
This book is manufactured in the United States of America

Acknowledgments

I am deeply grateful for support from the National Endowment
for the Arts and the Massachusetts Cultural Council, both of whom
provided fellowships that enabled me to continue work on this
manuscript. Thanks also to the MacDowell Colony for its generosity,
and for the wisdom of Ellen Bryant Voigt and of Jenny Barber, who
helped give shape to this material.

Acknowledgment is made also to the following publications
where some of these poems appeared, often in earlier versions.

Prairie Schooner ("Sammy Gordon," "That Wind" and "Painting Birdie")

Connecticut Review ("Fragment")

Boston Phoenix Literary Magazine ("Utility, A State of Grace")

Seneca Review ("On Her Wedding Day")

Barrow Street ("In the Details")

Artos Press: GRRR: An Anthology of Poem about Bears ("Called Back iv)

The Antigonish Review ("Potato" and "In the Common Room")

Birmingham Poetry Review ("Road")

Chachalaca Poetry Review ("The Limner")

In My Life: Encounters with the Beatles ("489 East 11th, Apt. 3C")

Salamander ("The Gift," "Nighthawks," and "Lamentation")

Poetpourri ("Field" and "Poem for My Son")

Pipsissewa ("Incunabulum")

Orpheus & Company: Contemporary Poems on Greek Mythology ("Aegis")

Word Thursdays: An Anthology ("Outside the Rail")

Natural Bridge ("Solitaire")

Fresh Ground ("Best Girl Room" and "God's Mercy")

Pedestal Magazine ("Covenant")

Poems for a Beach House (forthcoming) ("Dangerous Current")

Well Marcus better hang up your peace
give me your hand across the dark

—Zbigniew Herbert

Contents

III. CALLED BACK

/ 35

IV. ACROSS THE DARK

This is for Harry
and for Galen and Shea

POTATO

The thought lost in the eyes of a unicorn
appears again in a dog's laugh.

—Vladimir Holan,
translated from the Czech by Ian Milner

There are only two or three human stories,
and they go on repeating themselves as fiercely
as if they had never happened before.

—Willa Cather

the one sure thing

Mother prepared them every night,
mashed or boiled; they were
the quiet one on the plate,
the one sure thing.
Before supper, as she stood
at the sink to scrub and peel,
to watch wind sweep
the back meadow into cowlicks,
she filled our poor, lopsided
kitchen with something
urgent: the fragrance
of that small death in her hands.
I forgave her everything—
the broad column of her body
turned inward, toward
her task—as I leaned hungrily
against her leg, and she passed
down to me, a wedge, raw
and beaded with milk.

h a n d

A turtle so small it fit in the palm of my hand.
It worried surely forward, so as to be always arriving,
forged the cliffs of my fingers and the fjords between,
the slow forcemeat of will doing its work.
Kept in a tin box from my mother's kitchen.
All night miniature paws clawed at the insurmountable
fortress. I wanted to shout *run away!*
run! to its tiny thumb head, its four-poster
body, but knew no way to imagine a life
except to plunder the possibility of freedom.
Soon it was off its lettuce and slugs, and on the fifth

day it died. I dug deep in a clearing of pokeberries
to bury it. A stand of pine kept watch all winter
from far off across that meadow, where
each morning at dawn ring-necked pheasant
made their rounds, a cock and his four hens.
Water seeped up through the ground
that spring and stayed. Dragonflies skimmed
the calm surface; under a ribbed helmet of clouds
swamp beetles clung to the tracery of bittersweet
on the banks. By summer the pond
seemed it had always been there.

w a l l p a p e r

The Hartford-New Haven screams
past the Wire Mill; the dog yaps
and circles a chicken out of its pen.
Under Byzantine arches of birch
a child leans in at the hip of tree
in the early evening umbrage,
covers her eyes and counts to ten;
the others screech and scatter—while
inside the clapboard house
another child lies silently,
as the moon of the longest night
ignites her wallpaper—fence and trellis,
fence and trellis—beyond the gate
three sheep graze, heads bowed
to millet and broomcorn grinding
their blunt brown teeth. Clack
of father's buckle, rasp of zipper.
His buttocks calve in the dim light.
Her shoes wait by the bed for morning.

t h a t   w i n d

i

The night my mother was born wind
lifted the barn roof and set it down whole
in a field a mile across town—where sweetcorn
swooned up from mosaic flatland, windrows
of hedge apples pitching leeward.

And when she confides her longing
to return to the place where, when things turned
dangerous, she spiraled inward
to the dark of the canning cellar, its windows
like portals, the house a ship
creaking above her, to smell the wind

raking the prairie—I bring her back
to wave upon wave of corn leaves,
arched and ripe and so precisely arranged
the idea of it won't hold still—
The sun warms her broad face
and ordinary dress, her body rooted, finally,

in its proper hemisphere. I call to her
where she stands, a slim finger
on the horizon, and when she turns, her eyes
are afloat in their sockets. All my life
I have wanted that wind to mean this.

ii

And because nothing escaped her father's
domain, when the storm passed he
searched for the roof, which now
looked oddly perfect where it lay,
as though the barn had sunk
suddenly to its rafters into that field—
and finding it, took it apart board by board
with a plunderer's imprecision.

iii

Now a riot of moths rises
above the heat. Sawflies and digger wasps
thrum their hinged, transparent wings.
From a welter of redtop, gentian,
and goat's rue, a wood thrush appears,
milky throat glistening.

Nothing rests here that remembers—
not the fireweed, nor the chicory, nor
the Queen Anne's lace, its precise, dark center
a tiny, distant planet—where leafhoppers
hum and the foxtail and timothy lean:
a tyranny of cathedrals.

in the details

Inside wool mittens her small fingers
must have curled, thumbnails scoring perfect
crescent moons. Where she fell, just an empty
galosh, like a black bladder, in mud.
I'd been walking toward a white house
beyond the clearing, hadn't heard her

shouting for me to hurry or seen the struggle—
which, from where I was, I might have
mistaken for a casual ruffling of wings, her dark
scarf flapping among the lavender and sedge,
the man having crouched to wait for her there.

She'd been making her way home from school,
her tiny coat opened to the rain, one white sock
pulled up to bare knee. Slung over her shoulder,
thudding on her back with each step, a satchel—
inside it, bits of cheese and bread her mother
had packed that morning, hardening.

lamentation

Come closer, let me
tell you: I wasn't always a thief,
though when I was a boy I ate hungrily
from my neighbor's orchard.

As a man I was untidy.
Upon arriving I found always I had gone
too far. When asked my opinion
I'd shift one foot to the other.

The pleasure of death
will be to lie down again.

painting birdie

The women have each claimed an easel,
have put on their pastel smocks and now worry
the buttons through their holes. Under the high window
of the arts and crafts room at the Willowbrook Home
for the Disadvantaged, the teacher
says we're going to paint Birdie today, and Margaret

squeals Birdie! and claps her hands. Margaret
loves more than anything to stand at the easel
with a brush full of paint and hear her teacher
walk softly round the big room saying why worry?
When you paint Birdie you make a home
for her inside your painting. Here's the window

Birdie will be looking through, she says, tracing the window-
shaped edge of the canvas for Margaret.
So Margaret chooses blue for Birdie's home,
the fattest brushes from the easel
tray, and says to the blank canvas don't worry,
Birdie, I'll take care of you the way my teacher

takes care of me; you'll be safe here. Teacher
promises someday you'll come to the window.
Settling down to work she begins to worry
if the home might be big enough for herself, too—for Margaret—
so she paints, on the canvas propped on her wobbly easel,
two stick figures, herself and Birdie, and leaves the Home

for the first time, the only home
she's ever been inside. Good, very good, the teacher
praises, not seeing what Margaret sees on her easel—
herself and Birdie smiling out from their window—
and says why don't you paint them in a little, Margaret,
put clothes on them, and shoes. You'll worry

less if they're warm. But worry
she does as she paints and paints, over Birdie's new home,
shutting the window, drawing the shade, until Margaret
yells out we're lost! to the teacher
who's looking dreamily out the high window
into the blue forever above Margaret's easel,

and hasn't heard Margaret's worry, though no better teacher
has ever come to the Home or given the women a window
of hope, or Margaret a canvas and easel.

augury

i

It's true that Phillippe knew
something of families torn, so perhaps
he posed ours on this drab strip of beach
to convey a longing he could not speak:
how things might be held together
even against circumstance.

There's Londsberry's Store behind us,
and Sammy's house, and the Pioneer—
where Dad grilled hot dogs, made change
for the jukebox, seven days, seven nights—
perched on its spindly pilings, verticals
sinking into black and whiteness

with pleasing regularity beneath
a stippled August sky. Look
how we seem to have gathered
comfortably, each of us revealed
before we veer into separate lives:
Pat half-hiding behind Mother,

who holds me on her lap, Sue and Joanne
grinning back at the camera, and Paula,
with her wide smile, arms flung
around the neck of our father, who
sits on the sand alongside Mother
but does not touch her—perhaps

Phillippe had gently urged us into this
classic pose believing in the power of its
structure, the curved parallels of our tanned,
young arms, channeling along silent
meridians circling the earth, like
hoops of a barrel molding the staves,
before the dark floor of family
opened and we began the long fall.

i i

He was forty with a small child's mind.
Each morning at the front door
of their summer rental, his mother
wagged her finger up at Sammy's big face,
then straightened his Brooklyn Dodgers cap
before she sent him out to play.
In perfect weariness Mrs. Gordon
stood at the window to watch him,
as he looked carefully both ways
and crossed the street to the beach.
In striped tee shirt, brown lace-up shoes,
and oversized camp shorts, his legs
dropped like two pale posts.
He'd be laughing his man's laugh,
coarse, resonant, each intake of breath
hissing between his closed teeth.
My mother assured me he was harmless.
Holding in both hands his favorite toy, a pink
rubber beach ball, Sammy'd lope up and down
the shore in search of someone bigger than me
to play catch. Bathers recoiled in unison
until he was past—a human ripple
down the length of the little beach—
as if he were the god whose gaze
might wound them, or worse—though
inside his poor, stretched-out body
was just a terrible delicacy: a boy.

iii

The dangerous current could have
pulled us into the Sound, washed us up
dead on the dunes of Port Jefferson.
We were warned not to swim alone, and never
to Green Island, an acre of scrub pine
at high tide. Sometimes from the sea wall
fronting the old Waverly Hotel we'd
feel with our feet for the pipe, laid
along the ocean floor, that led out
to that island—line up on it,
the oldest and tallest of my sisters first,
and take it as far as we could, linked
hand to shoulder, the pipe descending
as it left shore, so that for a moment
we'd seem the same size. Youngest, and last,
I'd watch them as the water took in their
strong bodies to their chins and their heads
floated untethered. That day as I bobbed
backwards to shore so I never lost
sight of them, of all there was in the world,
the one farthest out yelled *I'm going to cross*,
her arms already rhythmic and sure,
her long legs scissoring just under the water.
The other three, in turn, looked
back at me, then followed.

SOLITAIRE

She measured to the hour its solitude.
She was the single artificer of the world
In which she sang. And when she sang, the sea,
Whatever self it had, became the self
That was her song, for she was the maker. Then we,
As we beheld her striding there alone,
Knew that there never was a world for her
Except the one she sang and, singing, made.

—Wallace Stevens

high window

Forming with my lips a taut *O*,
I take George Duffy's cock in my mouth—
take it all, he says, and I do, until my throat
closes around it rhythmically gagging
and he moans and pushes my head down harder
to his raised hips. I lift my eyes to see
through the window of his car, parked
after midnight in front of my house,

my mother playing solitaire
in the bay of her upstairs bedroom,
waiting for me to come in from my date,
her legs under the table negligible
as a ventriloquist's doll's, her left hand
holding the deck, her right
holding one card ready to play,

and my head bobs into the street light's
dull yellow and I know she will see me,
the way she's seen my older brother
fondle the neighbor boy's knee, in the kitchen,
while she peels the potatoes or garlics the roast—
any boy will do—and later, in the pantry,
while she dozes over the cards
in her tapestried wing chair, he'll smile,
perhaps, at how the little puckered anus
will spread and sometimes split.

Now, she's laid each card in its place—
win or lose it's the same—

and when I finish doing George Duffy
and he leans back, smiling, I let myself
out and walk toward my front steps, feeling
her eyes follow me from her high window—
my body, as I near the porch, falling away from
her view: foreshortened, diminished.

incunabulum

It seemed a tidy job—printing cardboard
merchandise signs for Malley's Department Store—
for a girl like me, prone to outbursts of sadness.
At first I was proud to slip my time card
into the clock, reassured by the thunk and specificity
of being present and accounted for.

I'd sit all day in a windowless eight feet
by eight feet of damp concrete, solvent
and Boraxo stiffening on my clothes,
working the store's ancient broadside roller press,
font drawer full of *News Gothic Bold*—
and fancy myself a monk, the Dark Ages

howling at the door, or Gutenberg fingering
his movable inventions. And though I struggled
against the buzz of boredom I'd sometimes
slump forward, lower my cheek to the press
bed, and sleep, my head crowning—incunabulum—

from a black desert of ink and typeface,
mouth opened as a cave is opened, the fire
inside banked down; when I woke, the buyer
from notions, her fists on her hips, was looking
down at me, the order she'd put in that morning—
Assorted Buttons 3 for 69¢—barely begun.

almanac

While father swirls his warm bouillon
with claret, and mother plucks a wild
dove for the evening meal, the child
lingers over the family's almanac,
inlaid with chips of mica,
fingering the phases of the moon,
the zodiac's naked man
showing which veins to open
under each of the twelve signs, fiery
suns of the four seasons, double suns
signaling the time to plant.
Wednesday's saint is the Blessed Benedict.
Today you may harvest chervil,
pimpernel, borage, and peas—

s t a n d   o f   t r e e s

i

In the wind sweeping across the bay from town
black-winged gulls swoop and dive in decisive arcs.
Sandpipers skitter on their slender reeded legs
along the unstable shoreline; snow
has settled in for the long haul.
On a thicket of bayberry, a tatter of kite, its tail
still attached, fitful in the sun's brief sting—
And beyond the thicket, farther down this barrier
island: the trees—so close now everything
falls from them, the world this side or that
of their mottled trunks; above, a cowl of naked
branches, the sky a silver medallion
tossed into the shivering air.

i i

The scrub pines take whatever comes.
When the sea breaches the beach road,
they spiral out of the reckless waves,
smoothed by the wind's relentless tongue.
They've no work but survival, the fierce
loneliness of sunset's theater drawn clean and hot
along the edge. If at times I am a useless mark—
a stone stung blind in its frozen socket of sand—
I am today where I ought to be,
or the whole of it would be diminished—
and never wanting to lose this place of mind
will not bring it back once it has gone
to wherever these certainties go.

on her wedding day

In the heat of her childhood
room, my mother, fifteen and pregnant,
turns away from the eyes of her father
who leans slackjawed against the doorjamb,
to hold her gaze on the Currier & Ives—
a blizzard of skaters arm in arm
banking their frozen pond. She struggles
with the corselette, guaranteed
to reduce her figure or her money back:
boned and covered with satin, silk garters
dandling. She's tugged it past her thighs,
and slowly, with great care, kneads her
belly into the field of elastic and lace,
working the garment up and finally
over her swelling breasts—a faint ring
of talc surrounds her on the carpet—
and now cinches the front stays so
tightly her torso is rigid, ungiving. Flesh
curls mid-back like the lip of a vase.

dürer's self-portrait as christ

Though even his dog is deceived,
scolded for licking his master's
painted visage, he sets the mirror
aside—his own face in reverse—to begin.
With synchrony and proportion,

one eye to the other, he girds his soul
against its betrayer—smoothes
his over-long nose to fit the face
of the Savior, shrouds the protruding ears—

those muscular flowers—with ringleted,
shoulder-length hair. Now Dürer
fingers his fur-collared robe, waits
eternal salvation. Gone
the churlish forebear retreating
in the dark behind the glass.

last day in aix

A sobbing so without modesty, I think at first she is acting—.
I'm meandering through the Old Town, irritable at the
thought of having to leave this country. Under the canopy
of plane trees along Cours Mirabeau, a man, with a forced
expression of indifference, is struggling to hold her limp body
up: a dead weight. He is dragging her, trying all the while to
get a better grip, her howl flung from the gut. The man, who
might be lover, or father, or simply a stranger nearby when
she'd needed help, reaches a side street, and there, in the gutter,
as he steadies himself and spreads his legs for balance, begins
to fold her like a map—knees and hips collapsing, head drooping,
her forehead hitting the street hard but making no sound—.
She's fetal now, except her bare arms which lie motionless on
the medieval cobblestones, gracefully splayed and useless.
I approach them and stand looking down, my arms flat at my
sides. Her howl persists and deepens. Raising her head, she
lets go a kind of squall, a puling yelp that reaches animal pitch.
No one on the street moves, except an aproned waiter outside
the corner café, who crooks his neck down the alley, holds his
gaze on them briefly, turns back to me, then shrugs.

t h a t g o d

My sister stands at the back of Saint Mary's
church in the taffeta wedding dress she's sewn,
puffed eyelet sleeves and pearl buttons—
tea length would be appropriate for the occasion
the etiquette book had said—Mother's
cameo pinned to a black velvet choker, white
cloche snug over her Dutch boy haircut.

And while nervously adjusting her gloves,
she glances sidelong down the aisle to where
the boy she's loved since second grade
waits for her—to the red cushions where
they'll kneel outside the rail, cordoned
from a priest preparing sacrament—
and the god who's bargained to meet them
halfway, the souls of their future
children thrown in for good measure.

under trinity church

From a hybrid of histories, Trinity
raises its masoned, medieval arm—a Spanish tower—
crenelated, turreted, crowning the foundation
of a massive Latin cross. On the west wall of the vaulted
nave, Christ, in leaded cobalt and papery slices
of alabaster, his outsized eyes like fine oysters.

Below him, sunk to bedrock and unseen for a century,
thousands of wooden pilings, like fingers rising up
into the landfilled bay of the River Charles, their tips
balancing the Roxbury pudding stone,
red Dedham granite, the freestone cutwork—
Quarries were mined, the tops of the three
hills of Boston brought by wagonload.

Here, the Massachuset fanned out their fishweirs.
Cradleboards on their backs, the women harvested
the trapped haddock, and in turn, the English
resettled the tribe in praying towns: Natick,
Ponkapoag, Pequot—fines were leveled for unchristian
behavior, five shillings for idleness, ten

for killing lice between the teeth. And farther back,
within the vast continent of Pangaea,
the Atlantic opened and closed and opened again,
widening finally to ocean, where
arrow worms and chordates thrived,
and the human phylum commenced—

Bereft above the transept of the church, Isaiah
gathers in his robe, in a time when even

the wilderness had a name: Moab, Zin—
As we adjust our hats, Paul, inhabiting one spandrel
of the east wall, seems caught in speech.
Only Moses, the Lawgiver, returns our gaze,
in a world, for the moment, set to rights,
while another goes silently, ineluctably, on.

t r a i n

What? one man asks,
and the other repeats a little louder,
Do you want a sandwich from the club car?—
then, another *What?*
In their voices, the tick of fatigue.

Now, he returns to his seat,
carrying with both hands a cardboard
snack tray: chips and styrofoam cup.
With each lurch sidewards he seems prodded—
an animal in a laboratory maze—

can't seem to steady himself, or free a hand
to grab the overhead bin, or adapt to the shunting.
I watch until our eyes meet, then look away.
Outside, a bachelor herd of junked cars,
untouched as heirlooms, rusted, Americana.

A factory. *Jenkins Valve. Since 1864.*   Abandoned.
Then the three-deckers, pink and turquoise;
half-moon copper windows squat on tar roofs.
On one, a mattress wilts over a back porch railing.
Everything takes on the shape of its neglect.

349 east 11th, apt 3c

Cabbies dropped us at 14th and Avenue A
refusing to drive into the neighborhood.
Roaches crawled on our toothbrushes.
How we loved that apartment.

We'd mimic the whiny voice
of our landlord in his bad black toupee,
the neighborhood men's dreamy rage—
stalking, on the hottest summer evenings,

some potent idea of themselves—the cats'
lewd and pitiable cries. We walked
twenty-seven blocks to the Chelsea Theater
for the Beatles double feature,

returning night after night until
we'd been there nineteen times—the man
in the ticket booth never once looked up—
we memorized every word of both films

and clowned the parts on the way home.
Sunk into our busted velvet sofa,
like the fleshy pulp of some great red fruit,
we'd spread the map of the world between us,

calculate the distance to everywhere else.
And when you touched my breasts
something in me let go—
the sad work of my childhood over.

CALLED BACK

And heaven is a different thing,
Conjectured, and waked sudden in—
And might extinguish me!

—Emily Dickinson

i

From the kingdom of ice,
in languorous perpetuity, the comet falls—
accretion of debris, the nucleus
a small city across. Sheets of dross
shift their aspect, emerge

and dissipate leeward.
In the solar wind, eons
and fearsome heat; a fragment
the size of a house breaks off.
Vanguards and outriders are blown

back, a handful of seed broadcast
across the sky. We take what we need
from the night—some grace,
some inexplicable bounty
rushing headlong into our sight.

ii

November rains on the benches.
Swan boats that glide in the warm months
have been hauled out for storage; somewhere
their delicte necks are arched in a row.
Now the hawthorns drop their rare leaves,
staining the walk with shadow leaves.

iii

Not dead as much as caught
in a terror passed on to them—
The coelacanth, preserved
within a tank fashioned just
to fit; kestrels and goshawks
stare with identical glass eyes.
The fruit bat, rigged in place, descends
forever into its painted diorama.
Only the dust shimmering
along the eland's spiraled horn
advances. As for us:
no habitat, no reconstructed life.
Facing forward—discrete, separate—
we are tagged and classified
in the terrible dryness.

i v

This small found bear, rescued
from a dumpster, oblivion
of the once-loved, brought
to the studio and wrapped in gauze
from blunt feet to just below
blue plastic eyes, dipped
then dipped again in beeswax
to cover the slip-stitched mouth,
the black felt nose, which hardened
to thick, yellowed skin over
a hand-sized bear, arms and legs
hushed, only the eyes unpossessed—
and in this mute countenance,
a grief so arched in necessity
it has begun to fall away.

v

This spring is worse than last—
the brambles have outflanked the quince,
making the best of exile
on the side hill. I work my way

down the prickered branches,
but it's the same old argument.
The base is thick as a wrist
and my shears balk. Something

is released in the hard lesson, here,
at the root. I admit defeat.
I'm afraid dying won't demand this
struggle: the best in me called back.

ACROSS THE DARK

We do not see things as they are,
we see things as we are.

—The Talmud

j o i n e d

Two infant heads with three arms and two legs,
preserved at the Muséum National d'Histoire Naturelle
for the nineteenth century appetite—
Then, a pair of males: one head, one well-formed
brain, two legs and rudiments of two more. And here,

two full upper bodies are joined at the base
from which a pair of perfect legs extend: a tidy dialectic.
In the adjoining case, a female, one head at each
end of a joined spine. Does one perceive the other
as it is itself perceived—not as in a mirror
but cleaving to self-concealment?

This one's nearly normal, yet a tiny headless brother
projects from his chest: *an imperfect twin*
the wall text reads. I fix on the lump on the back
of my hand, like a miniature self rising up
from under the vast organ of my skin, and wonder
which of us might be the imperfect one; and what it is
she needs to tell me that I need to know.

On the disposable, the forsaken, Jerome
paints with nail polish and white-out,
tapping the excess from his brush

like monks once tapped their quills
on the lip of the ink horn;
Portrait of Charles

on a crushed bottle cap, mortared
with his own clipped toenails
and a dead lover's ashes.

The body offers its currency—
(He was once a boy hiding
in the laundry basket,

wearing his mother's slip, curled
as a filigreed illumination, waiting
for his path to be translated—)

The great paw of the virus blinding him,
he fashions a spin board game
with objects of his passion:

mirror, eyeliner, rouge—and names it
what a woman no longer needs.
Queen of the drag queens, Jerome

puts all things to use—utility is a state of grace—
rendering in miniature a cult of relics.
And when his gallery advises him

to work larger, he paints *The Last Supper*
on the shell of an almond—
each disciple's body a betrayal.

the limner

To make a likeness from particulars—
a startle of lace, swag of damask
with tassel—he paints
portraits for a meal, or a bed,

traveling the Post Road out of Boston.
The shipwright's daughter folds
her stout fingers on her lap, sets
her lantern jaw. Dust floats

from the window in a bar of light
as afternoon passes, illuminating
his muddied jackboots.
                              What is essential here

has no face, only the limner
and his sleepy poser, sheep's bladders
full of lampblack and Prussian blue.
On the table, some bread, a knife.

best girl

Men who laid track
for the Atlantic & Pacific
from Flagstaff west to California
homed in like cattle, twenty a night.
She'd unbutton their stiffened
breeches and open her robe to them—
tussock of hair between her legs,
salt sour dominion. One man
asked for fresh water in a basin
before burrowing his face there.

Above the haloed shadow of gas light,
a painting of winter trees—snow quiet,
unpeopled: some daydream, hovering—
And when he finished with her he
penciled on the wall above the bed,
in a wide, childish scrawl—
RH from SC April 1899.
A good time was had here by me.

like this

From the sidewalk I can see the soda jerk
drying a mug, setting it down
on a cloth-covered shelf, the counter
curving like the prow of a great wooden boat
carrying the earth's souls. A fly

probes a drop of milk that's let go
from the lip of a pitcher. At Phillies
the coffee is dark and bitter. The fall of light
from the ceiling fixture remains constant.
Neither happiness nor unhappiness settles

on the chromed napkin dispensers,
the condiment trays of relish and pickles.
Most of the stools are empty.
The man with his back to the street
is adrift in the acid green of the far wall.

He places his hat on the seat beside him,
stirs a second spoonful of sugar into his coffee.
Through the adjacent wall of glass, beyond
his reflection, a store front implodes in darkness,
its tier of orthopedic shoes half in shadow.

In the upstairs flat, lights have gone out.
Against indifference, will and destiny
make their truce. We are bound,
too, like this: bowsprit to stem
above a sea of unwanting.

w h i t e

On the long sweep of barren road
that heads from our town to the next,
salt marsh on one side, cranberry bog
on the other, a boy you grew up with

hit a tree. Going ninety the grocer said.
Died instantly, thank god.
You played basketball with the boy

in second grade; in our kitchen
you'd both try to jump high enough
to touch the door jamb. He always won.

In winter the boundary
between the towns, crossing that road,
becomes clearly marked where snow plows
pull up their blades—a sudden ridge of white—
intangible, gone by morning.

s i l k

I was where you knew I'd be
brushing my doll's real hair,
fingering the blanket's silk.
Keep still, you said
as you closed the door
to my dormered room
behind you and reached
for the bedpost, pawing
the dark as you neared.
Keep still. This won't take long.
A stealth gunner, you pinned
your target and locked on.
No intervals no let up—

c o v e n a n t

On the falconer's leathered fist she bows
straight between her tethered, green gold
legs, thrusts her beak into the grouse,
then bolts straight up with each morsel
before it is lodged in her crop
and with a sinuous toss, swallowed.

It's not faith that brings him to her
to covet her singular hunger, this
thrall at arm's length—grace and grief
on the gauntlet—but some imperative
that accumulates across his shoulders
when, sated, she stretches her long wing.

t r u t h

White coat flapping, Dr. Howland
unlocks the ward door and hurries to a seat,
clicks his ballpoint pen, and without
looking up says, good morning, people,
who wants to start? Marion clears her throat,
lets her book drift gently to her lap,
thumb keeping her place.
During free time, we play truth

as the shapeless afternoon hangs plumb,
drag vinyl chairs around the coffee table
into a tight circle. None of us ever lies.
When I ask Marion if she believes
God knows she's in here, she replies,
of course, but God loves only Catholics,
and leaning in until our bare knees touch, says,
he doesn't even know *you're* alive.

m e r c y

Someone announced one morning at group
that we were going to talk about God's mercy
as we all sat in the common room
on folding chairs lining the four walls
as if thrown by centrifugal force:—

Fran, who'd wept all night in the next bed,
her closed curtain translucent in the bald light
from the corridor; —Carla, always begging a cigarette,
and that woman who hadn't left her house
for eight years before she was brought in

wrapped in a blanket. And that leering,
wind-up-toy of a man—when we heard
his slippers shuffling behind us
we'd cross our arms over our breasts
so he couldn't get at them.

I made my first drawing for you, a small boat
moored to an impossibly slender dock,
while we watched the nurses dole out
our night meds into tiny, fluted cups.
When the doctor asked what you most desired,

you said you wanted to be me, to live *my* life,
when all that was left of it was morning fading
to lights out, and morning again. No one

came to visit you until your mother
appeared one day in the ward lunchroom.

Something seemed gone from her.
She held a small basket of fruit.
Oh, Nilda, your black hair opened all the doors;
freedom rose from the brocade of your voice.
You led me out into the kind of cold
that was hard to breathe.

d a r k n e s s

Blackout. A city lies prone.
The bartender at the Gordian Knot
stops his mechanical conversation,
follows his regulars out onto the avenue.
The backup trio at the Five Spot
keeps jamming in the dark.
Dropping into the canyons
of Madison and Park, elevators
sigh to a stop. Along 59th,
where hackberry and Oriental pine
once thrived, shoppers scatter like ants
on the concrete skin of the city.

From seven hundred miles of subway
tunnels, netherworld crisscrossing
under the five boroughs, where
Norway rats stop for nothing,
from caverns and viaducts,
abandoned and moldering—that place
of darkness prevailing—he ascends,
battle weary and frayed in corselet
and muscled breastplate, into a night
so clear the Great Galaxy spirals beyond
Andromeda, his pilum fixed at his side,
his eyes gold as a snow leopard's: a silence
illuminated, visible, at last.

o f   s a l t

The good fisherman lifts the lid
of the chest, set adrift among the Cyclades,
to find a boy and his mother
in each other's arms. Everything
is about to be asked of this boy.

Danaë stretches her long legs, drinks
greedily from the fisherman's flask.
The boy does not uncurl himself
from their tiny floating pod, but remains
there through the long night, alone,

fingering the ridge of salt, the swollen wood
where Danaë's hips had been lodged.
Go on, then, Perseus. Much is to be done.
They've polished the helmet of invisibility,
stitched the purse to hold the Gorgon's head.

Wake into your life, where you'll float
on your ankle plumes, and dance
with the trickster king, where
you'll get to keep nothing—
not even the shoes on your feet.

s i l e n c e

Tonight, at room 322, left of the elevator,
we fumble with the key card, undress
in silence. On TV, a scientist from Harvard,
whose passion could make you weep,
gives us black holes and reasonable
assumptions. We lie like two particles bound
in theoretical space, the forces between us hidden,
trees beating at the edge of our rented room.

The solar wind that means to bend us now
was there in New York, when we were new lovers,
and I stepped away from you onto a balcony
promising a view of the whole city.
If I'd wanted I could have touched
the Brooklyn Bridge, dipped my arm
into the East River, reached uptown
to the Williamsburg, the Queensboro.
Pivoting, I began to coax you out,
but you'd stiffened against the door jamb.
It was not for yourself you feared,
you said, but that your voice might
knock me over the balcony's ledge.
How we've come to trust

such things, these calculations, as though
we might not understand all at once

that the deep chords of premonition
are located simply in narrowing fields
of possibilities. Once on the Cross
Bronx Expressway, someone—had she
intended to change the structure of the world?—
walked across three lanes of traffic to
the cement median to spray paint on it
the single word *road*.

Notes

under trinity church: The church, designed by Henry Hobson Richardson and completed in 1877, is located in Copley Square, Boston.

called back (i):   This poem was inspired by the succession of comets Hyakutaki and Hale Bopp.

called back (iv):   My friend and colleague Lorey Bonante created this sculpture. This poem is dedicated to her.

called back (v):   *Called back*, in the last line, were the last words Emily Dickinson wrote. They are engraved on her tombstone.

joined: The Muséum National d'Histoire Naturelle is in Paris, France.

utility, state of grace: The character of Jerome is loosely based on Jerome Caja, an artist and actor, who died of AIDS in 1995. The line *utility is a state of grace* is borrowed from Jerome's friend, and mine, novelist Adam Klein.

the limner: A limner was an itinerant portrait painter during 18th- and 19th-century America.

like this: Inspired by Edward Hopper's painting entitled "Nighthawks."

of darkness: Marcus Aurelius, to whom the Herbert epigraph on the title page also refers, was a second-century Roman emperor. His life was an expression of ironic conflict; though engaged throughout his reign in warfare on all Roman fronts, he sustained a deep and passionate belief in Stoicism, whose philosophy, markedly different from the contemporary connotation, embodied an indwelling rational principle, a wholly individual moral purpose. He wrote the *Meditations* while encamped with his army on the Danube.

covenant: Only female falcons can successfully be trained for the sport of falconry.

Pam Bernard, a poet and painter from Boston, Massachusetts, holds a BA from Harvard University and an MFA in Creative Writing from the Program for Writers at Warren Wilson College. Ms Bernard's most recent awards are a second Massachusetts Cultural Council Fellowship in Poetry, a MacDowell Fellowship, and a National Endowment for the Arts Fellowship in Creative Writing. Her previous collection of poems, published by Bright Hill Press, is entitled *My Own Hundred Doors*. She teaches writing at Emerson College and Northeastern University, Boston.